The 30 Seconds Method

OrangeBooks Publication

1st Floor, Rajhans Arcade, Mall Road, Kohka, Bhilai, Chhattisgarh 490020

Website: **www.orangebooks.in**

© Copyright, 2024, Author

All rights reserved. No part of this book may be reproduced, stored in a retrieval system, or transmitted, in any form by any means, electronic, mechanical, magnetic, optical, chemical, manual, photocopying, recording, or otherwise, without the prior written consent of its writer.

First Edition, 2024

ISBN: 978-93-6554-107-6

THE 30 SECONDS METHOD
UNBEATABLE SALES TACTICS

RAJ ADGOPUL

OrangeBooks Publication
www.orangebooks.in

Preface

A Journey from Survival to Mastery in Face-to-Face Sales

Imagine stepping off a crowded train in the heart of Mumbai, with nothing in your pocket but a determination to make a life in a city that does not stop to breathe. I learned sales the hard way- not from books, but from the streets, platforms, and teeming high streets of Mumbai, where every interaction felt like a battle between survival and hunger. I did not start with any special insight or talent. I was in many ways a 'village idiot' thrown into one of the busiest cities in the world, where a single wrong step could knock you down and leave you lying on the ground as thousands walked past without a second glance.

'Your personality reflects your life experiences.'

The truth is, my life depended on reading people, on figuring out the subtle cues they gave off before they even said a word. From selling T-shirts in narrow lanes of Mumbai slums to eventually, fine jewellery in shops across the UK, I realized that whether you are on the high street or in a high-end shop, human instincts don't change. People operate on autopilot, often led by ancient instincts and automatic reactions they are not even aware of. I began to understand that it is possible to tap into this blind-spot territory, not by manipulating people, but by creating a genuine connection that triggers something real within them.

'The human brain's blind spots are where trust can be built or broken.'

This book is a guide to mastering the ancient, instinctual language of human interaction. We are going to delve into the psychology that predates civilization itself- the hunter-gatherer instincts that drive us, and the unspoken signals that make us trust, like, or avoid someone. These are the same instincts that helped our ancestors navigate survival in small tribes and that we, oddly enough, still carry into the modern world, even though life has evolved beyond anything they could have imagined.

'Humans evolved to trust those in close proximity who were offering value, not taking it.'

What if you could make a lasting impression within 30 seconds of meeting someone? What if, by understanding subtle cues, blind spots, and human psychology, you could build trust almost instantly? I know, it sounds a little like science fiction. But here is the thing: human beings are hardwired to connect. We are drawn to comfort, safety, and trust, and if you understand how to cultivate these emotions, you can bring a stranger to engage with you as if you were an old friend.

'The first 30 seconds in a face-to-face interaction determine everything.'

Through a series of lessons, stories, and exercises, I'll show you how to:

- Master the psychology of proximity and why it's so important to build trust in close encounters.

- Recognize and respond to blind spots in the brain that create space for genuine connection.

- Engage the subconscious 'hunter-gatherer brain' in every interaction so you come across as a friend, not a threat.

- Build core confidence that goes beyond situational bravado, carrying you with a natural sense of ease, even under pressure.

'Good business is done with heart and authenticity.'

So, as we embark on this journey together, prepare to look at interactions differently. Be ready to try a few bold moves on the high street, maybe some unusual techniques in conversation, and discover how the hidden wiring of the brain- the part that has kept us alive for thousands of years- can be your greatest ally.

'The truth always shines through; you can't fake authenticity.'

Let's unlock the art of human connection, where the science of survival meets the heart of business.

Ready to transform the way you approach every interaction? Let us begin.

Index

Chapter 1: Mumbai - A Crash Course in Survival and Adaptability
- The High Street Shuffle: An Experiment in Human Blind Spots
- Arrival in Mumbai: The Train Incident
- Oh! The helium balloon
- Survival Skills and Building Awareness of Subtle Cues

Chapter 2: Ancient Instincts in Modern Sales
- Prehistoric Psychology and the Hunter-Gatherer Mindset
- The Evolution of Projectile Weapons and Blind Spots
- Friend or Enemy? Navigating Trust and Threat in Close Proximity

Chapter 3: Understanding Proximity and Creating Connection
- The Psychology of Proximity: Activating the Archaic Brain
- Non-Threatening Presence and Disarming Defences
- Building Instant Trust Through Comfort and Familiarity

Chapter 4: The 30-Seconds Sales Interaction
- The First Five Seconds: Creating Distraction and the 'Something Else' Frame
- Five Seconds of Pitching and the Expected 'No'
- The False Time Constraint: Willingness to Walk Away
- Final Ten Seconds: Inviting Engagement and Broadcasting Hooks
- The Fishing Analogy: Letting Go of Attachment to Outcomes

Chapter 5: Frames and the 'Something Else' Frame
- The Dinner with Friends Analogy: Switching Frames
- Three Key Frames: Known, Sales, and Something Else
- Practical Application of Frame Psychology in Face-to-Face Sales

Chapter 6: Inside Your Head vs. Outside Your Head
- Trust Sparks Connection
- Inside the Head: Self-Monitoring, Fears, and Insecurities
- Outside the Head: Comfort, Confidence, and Attunement
- A James Bond story
- Shortcut to Trust: Creating Comfort and Safety for Others

Chapter 7: Conquering Fear with Core Confidence
- Fear as an Emotional Response to Thoughts
- Situational Confidence vs. Core Confidence
- The Thermometer Analogy for Stable State of Mind
- Exercises for Developing Core Confidence

Chapter 8: Offering Value Through Genuine Connection
- Authentic Interactions: Providing Value without Taking
- The Fishing Analogy Revisited: Embracing Abundance
- Cultivating Rapport and Connection by Letting Go of Agenda

Chapter 9: Calibration and the Art of 'Being' Over 'Doing'
- The 95% Body Language, 5% Words Principle
- Internalizing Knowledge for Natural Calibration
- The Spider-Man Slow-Motion Effect: Enhanced Perception
- Final Exercise: Practicing Authenticity and Alignment

Conclusion: Bringing It All Together with Heart and Humanity

- Reflecting on Prehistoric Humanity and Modern Civilization
- The Archaic Brain and the Need for Genuine Human Connection
- Selling with Heart: Why Business Done with Heart is More Secure
- Takeaway: Honouring Human Instincts and Practicing the Art of Connection

Introduction

Let me tell you a secret about people: we are all pretending. Every single one of us. We put on masks to navigate life, whether it's the polite small talk of an English tea party or the unspoken bargains of a Mumbai marketplace. Beneath those masks, we're all wired the same way- we crave connection. And those first 30 seconds of any interaction? That's when we decide if someone's worth connecting with or not.

Take the English, for example. They've elevated the art of pretending to near perfection. Need a dose of human interaction but don't want to admit it? Join a club. From knitting to pram racing to cheese rolling, there's a club for every interest. But make no mistake- these aren't just quirky hobbies; they're socially acceptable ways to get your interaction fix without looking needy. It's genius.. You get your connection and your plausible deniability in one tidy package. If you are English (familiar with English culture) as a reader you will know exactly what I am talking about, but the rest of the world likely will not understand!

Now contrast this with India, where pretending is optional, and connection is an unspoken rule of survival. In the bustling streets of Mumbai, where life hurtles along at breakneck speed, you don't have time to mask your intentions. Every chai seller, shopkeeper, and commuter knows how to read you in an instant. It's not just about selling or surviving- it's about understanding people on a level so instinctive; it almost feels magical.

I learned this lesson early, at a village fair. I was nine years old, clutching ten rupees. I'd saved over months. I bought a shiny red helium balloon, thinking it was the most magical thing in the world- until I saw the stalls of sweets and toys I could no longer afford. In desperation, I tried selling the balloon to anyone who'd listen. No one bought it. That day, I learned an interesting lesson: the manner in which you start any interaction matters. Those first words, those first seconds, set the tone for everything that follows.

Years later, I arrived in England with just £5 in my pocket and a head full of dreams. I didn't know it then, but I'd go on to build a six-figure business selling jewellery across the UK, but the lessons I'd learned in Mumbai stayed with me. From going to bed hungry in the slums to walking confidently into boutiques in the Cotswolds, one thing remained constant: success always came down to making people feel seen, valued, and connected in those first few moments.

This book is your guide to mastering those moments. Drawing from my journey across two wildly different worlds, it blends ancient instincts with modern insights, teaching you how to create trust, spark curiosity, and leave a lasting impression. Whether you're breaking the ice with a shopkeeper in Jaipur, starting a conversation in a London boutique, or making your pitch on a global stage, the techniques here will help you stand out in a way that feels effortless and real.

We'll explore everything from the psychology of connection to the art of humour, the subtle cues that build trust, and the quirks of English clubs. Because if you can make someone, feel like they're part of something- whether it's a balloon sale, a cheese-rolling contest, or a brilliant new idea- you've already won.

Content

Chapter - 1
Mumbai - A Crash Course in Survival and Adaptability 1

Chapter - 2
Ancient Instincts in Modern Sales 7

Chapter - 3
Understanding Proximity and Creating Connection 10

Chapter - 4
The 30-Seconds Sales Interaction 14

Chapter - 5
Frames and the 'Something Else' Frame 20

Chapter - 6
Inside Your Head vs. Outside Your Head 23

Chapter - 7
Conquering Fear with Core Confidence 27

Chapter - 8
Offering Value Through Genuine Connection 30

Chapter - 9
Calibration and the Art of 'Being' Over 'Doing' 33

Conclusion
Bridging the Archaic and the Modern with Heart 36

Chapter - 1
Mumbai - A Crash Course in Survival and Adaptability

Introduction: From a Village Idiot to Sales Maverick

A Quick Experiment Before We Begin

Before diving into the book, let's start with a small experiment that'll give you a quick taste of what's to come. Next time you're out on a busy street, try this: as someone walks toward you, hold their gaze for just a moment. Notice which direction their eyes flick- to the left or right. Without even realizing it, their body will usually follow wherever their eyes go. So, if you're trying to avoid the awkward 'which-way-are-you-going' dance, simply step in the opposite direction.

Why does this trick work? It reveals a fascinating blind spot in our brains. We operate on autopilot far more than we realize. This eye-flick dance, like so many interactions, shows how we rely on instinctive reactions- ones that have been hardwired into us over thousands of years.

Take a few minutes to try this experiment the next time you're out. It's a playful exercise, but it hints at a deeper truth: mastering these hidden signals gives you an edge in connecting with others, in as little as 30 seconds.

Mumbai greeted me like a swift slap to the face—and I mean that quite literally.

It's a city that doesn't apologize, doesn't slow down, and most definitely doesn't wait for you to catch up. Coming from my small village, I might as well have landed on another planet. The noise, the people, the sheer pace- it was all overwhelming. I was nobody, and in a place like Mumbai, if you're nobody, life's simple: you either figure out how to swim, or you drown.

A Harsh Welcome

On my very first morning, eager to get to my new job, I found myself on a crowded railway platform, facing the infamous Mumbai local trains. Now, if you haven't experienced these trains, let me paint a picture for you. Thousands of people, all crammed into compartments, spilling out of doors, fighting for every inch of space. But here's the thing that struck me as odd- there were two compartments in front of me. One was packed so tightly I doubted anyone could breathe, while the other was nearly empty. It seemed obvious to me to choose the emptier carriage. I stepped in without a second thought, thinking I'd outsmarted the crowd.

> **'Your identity is like a seed—it shapes your thoughts, which guide your actions, and the feedback you get from others grows the cycle.'**

What I didn't know was that I'd walked into a first-class compartment, a place I didn't belong, as my ticket was for second class. Moments after boarding a large, scowling man grabbed my collar with surprising strength. He asked, "Do you have a first-class ticket?" Now, I'd never even heard of a 'first-class ticket,' much less understood what he was talking about. I barely managed to stammer out a response before his hand connected with my face.

In seconds, I was hurled out of the train, landing on the platform with one shoe gone, my 50 rupees watch broke, my shirt torn, and my pride bruised beyond repair. Thousands of people brushed past without a second glance. Mumbai didn't care. As I sat there on the dirty concrete, all I wanted was to go home. The city had shown me its teeth, and I wasn't sure I was ready to bite back.

But here's the thing: I didn't really have a choice. There *was* no easy way back. So, I stood up, dusted myself off, and made a promise: I would survive here, whatever it took, or I would die here and never go back to my village.

Learning to Read People

The slap was a wake-up call. In the days and weeks that followed, I quickly realized that to get by in Mumbai, I needed to learn to read people- and fast. How else could I know who would toss me to the floor like a rag, and who might listen to me and buy a T-shirt? This was a place where life moved at a relentless pace, and people weren't about to slow down for me. I began to pay attention to small cues, studying the way people moved, the expressions on their faces, and even the way they held their bags or looked at others around them. Every little detail counted, and every interaction felt like a matter of survival.

'Core value is the essence of your personality that you carry everywhere.'

In those first months, I developed an almost sixth sense, an ability to pick up on subtle signs, on shifts in body language that others might miss. It wasn't a skill I learned out of interest or curiosity- it was the only way I could survive.

I was living in a cramped space with 23 other people, scraping by on the few rupees I earned. My daily budget for food was the equivalent of seven pence, and there were nights I went to bed with my stomach growling, desperate for a meal I couldn't afford.

But hunger has a way of sharpening the mind. When you're that driven, when you're that hungry, you learn fast. I started to see patterns in people, in their behaviours. I could sense when someone was about to push past me on the street or if a shopkeeper was losing patience with my haggling. My survival depended on my ability to navigate these tiny moments, to understand people in a way that would keep me safe and help me get ahead.

Building Resilience and Awareness

I remember a moment on one of those cramped trains when it hit me- life here wasn't about brute strength; it was about resilience. Every day, I'd see people packed into those trains like sardines, yet still managing to smile, joke, and make it through. I realized that I was watching adaptability in its purest form. Mumbai didn't change for anyone.

After the train incident, I dusted myself off, both literally and emotionally, and made a vow to survive, no matter what. Mumbai had dealt me my first lesson in harsh realities, but it wasn't my first brush with the art of misjudging a situation- or the sting of getting it wrong.

That lesson came years earlier in my small village, far removed from Mumbai's chaos but no less brimming with its kind of challenges. I was nine years old, wide-eyed, and ready to take on the world- or at least the annual village fair. It was the highlight of the year, the only time our sleepy town came alive with colour, noise, and the irresistible smell of fried snacks.

You see, my first real encounter with 'sales' wasn't in a bustling train station. It was under the dusty tent of a helium balloon vendor- a man who would unwittingly teach me that what you say in the first few moments of a conversation can set the tone for everything that follows. And, let me tell you, I learned it the hard way.

The fair was the biggest event of the year in our little village- a riot of colours, sounds, and smells that drew crowds from miles around. As a nine-year-old boy clutching my precious ten rupees, saved painstakingly over months, I felt like a king stepping into his kingdom. For a kid growing up in the 1980s in a remote Indian village, ten rupees was a fortune. The fair was my chance to spend it on something spectacular.

As soon as I walked through the gates, there it was- the very first stall. Floating above the vendor's head were helium balloons, bright and shiny, shimmering like jewels in the sunlight. Back then, helium balloons were a novelty, almost magical. The vendor caught my eye, smiled, and held out a bright red balloon. "Ten rupees," he said, his voice dripping with charm.

It didn't even cross my mind to look around the rest of the fair. I handed over my entire fortune without hesitation. "Enjoy!" the vendor said, handing me the string like he was bestowing me with a treasure. For a moment, I was on cloud nine. The balloon floated above me, catching everyone's attention. I felt like the envy of every kid at the fair.

But as I wandered deeper into the fair, the magic began to fade. Stall after stall, I saw spinning tops that sparkled, wooden toys that clicked and clacked, and sweets that made my mouth water. My red balloon, once a prized possession, now felt like a bad investment. My heart sank. How could I have been so impulsive?

Determined to undo my mistake, I marched back to the vendor, balloon in hand. I stood there, trying to muster the right words. But when I finally opened my mouth, what came out was, "Bhaiyya, (brother) Will you buy it back?"

The vendor stared at me like I'd lost my mind. "Buy it back?" he asked, his voice rising in disbelief. "This isn't a shop! It's a stall! You bought it, it's yours."

"But I don't want it anymore!" I blurted, desperate. His face twisted into an annoyed grimace. "No refunds, no exchanges. Go enjoy your balloon," he snapped, waving me away.

I wasn't ready to give up. I stood there for the next three and a half hours, watching him sell balloon after balloon. Each time there was a lull, I'd try again. "Please, I'll take five rupees. Three? Anything!" But he refused to even look at me. The other vendors started to chuckle, amused by the stubborn kid who couldn't take no for an answer. I felt the heat of humiliation rising in my cheeks.

By the time I gave up, it was nearly midnight. But I wasn't done yet. I marched to my uncle's house, nearly an hour away, determined to make things right. When I arrived, I woke him up with a frantic knock on the door. My uncle opened it, bleary-eyed and confused. "What's wrong?" he asked.

"Will you buy this balloon?" I said, thrusting the string toward him.

"What?!" he exclaimed, trying to process what was happening.

"It's a helium balloon! Very rare! I paid ten rupees, but I'll sell it to you for five," I said, trying to sound like a seasoned salesman. My uncle burst out laughing. "Raj, it's the middle of the night! What am I going to do with a balloon?"

"But I don't want it anymore!" I said, my voice breaking with frustration.

My uncle shook his head, chuckling softly. "Raj, it's your balloon now. You made your choice. The best thing you can do is enjoy it while it lasts." He sent me off to bed, where I lay awake staring at the ceiling, clutching the string of my unwanted balloon.

By the time I left my uncle's house, it was three in the morning. I trudged home, exhausted and defeated, the balloon bobbing behind me like a cruel reminder of my foolishness. For the next year, every time I thought about the fair, regret gnawed at me. I imagined all the other things I could have bought, all the joy I could have had if I'd just thought before spending my precious ten rupees.

That year of regret taught me more than any adult's lecture ever could. I realized that the first words you say in any situation can dictate the entire outcome. My impulsive "Will you buy it back?" had set the wrong tone with both the vendor and my uncle. If I'd approached the vendor differently- maybe shared my story, explained my regret, and appealed to his kindness- perhaps things would've turned out differently.

> **'Good business is done with heart and authenticity.'**

It was my first lesson in communication and sales: how you open matters. Words have power, but it's not just what you say- it's how you say it, and the emotion you bring to the interaction. When I was nine, I didn't realize it, but that helium balloon marked my journey into understanding human connections, mastering first impressions, and the art of making my words count. After some time, I began to appreciate the city's rhythm. It wasn't just about reading people's faces or gestures anymore; it was about sensing their energy and feeling their intent. People operated on autopilot, driven by a survival instinct that had been refined over generations. Just like ancient hunters, they knew where to move, when to dodge, and how to avoid danger- all without thinking.

The more I observed, the more I understood that this wasn't just a lesson for survival in Mumbai; it was a lesson for life. People's actions, their choices, were influenced by something deep-rooted, something instinctual. It wasn't about logic or reason- it was about survival, about operating on a level of awareness most people didn't even know they had. And in a strange way, it was beautiful.

Chapter - 2
Ancient Instincts in Modern Sales

Theme: Leveraging Evolutionary Psychology for Authentic Connections

Introduction: Our Hunter-Gatherer Legacy

For most of human history, we lived in small tribes, rarely encountering strangers. The mind's priority was survival, and any stranger walking into our circle was automatically assessed for danger. Friend or enemy? Because making a wrong assessment literally meant the difference between life and death for our ancestors. That was the essential question. In those times, there was no room for in-depth analysis- our brains made snap judgments, instincts that linger even today.

When you approach a customer, their brain makes the same 'friend or enemy' decision, even if they don't realize it. But here's the key: you can influence this reaction without saying a word. Later, we'll explore the 'something else' frame- a way to position yourself as more than just another salesperson, instantly flipping their perception of you. In later chapters, we'll dig into the power of body language, subtle signals, and how to shift a person's perspective of you.

> 'In the hunter-gatherer era, people trusted based on non-threatening presence.'

The Psychology of Proximity: Connecting Without Triggering Defences

Before projectile weapons were invented, hunters had to get close to their prey, working with skill, subtlety, and precision. In the sales environment, this proximity principle means that the closer you get, the more they feel the need to decide if you're a friend or an enemy. Getting this right can make the difference between a warm welcome and a cold dismissal.

Think of it like a 'soft or light presence' - one that doesn't demand attention. In Chapter 5, we'll explore the 'something else' frame in detail, and see how it's the key to slipping past those defences and creating genuine engagement without pressure. You'll learn how specific techniques can help you blend into the interaction, making customers feel comfortable and curious.

> 'The human brain's blind spots are where trust can be built or broken.'

The Warm End vs. Cold End of the Pool: Finding Common Ground

Picture every interaction as a swimming pool. When you plunge into a hard sell, you're throwing the customer into the cold end, where defences rise. But if you approach with a different frame, you guide them into the warm end, a zone where they can engage with you as a human, not just a salesperson.

> 'People buy from people they like and trust'.

As the book unfolds, we'll talk about how to 'anchor' in this warm end, making customers feel naturally at ease and creating a space where the sale almost sells itself. And trust me, once you master this approach, you'll wonder how you ever worked without it.

Blind Spots: Operating Within the Customer's 'Mammoth' Mindset

Here's where we bring in the analogy of the woolly mammoth. Just like the ancient mammoth had physical blind spots that a hunter could use to get close without triggering its defences, the human brain has blind spots too- spaces where we operate on autopilot, unaware of every interaction. These are opportunities you can capitalize on, getting close without setting off alarms.

Imagine yourself as that hunter, but instead of weaponry, your tools are empathy and awareness. In Chapter 4, we'll break down how to use 'blind spot entry points' in your sales interactions. You'll learn how to stay in their peripheral, moving closer to the sale without putting up defences.

> 'Calibration is 95% body language and 5% words.'

Practical Application: The Hunter's Approach

In the hunter-gatherer era humans relied on subtlety, observation, and timing. Good hunters didn't approach prey head on- they found the perfect angle, entered quietly, and remained in a 'safe' space. You can apply this to sales by adopting a gentle energy that registers as neutral or positive to the customer's subconscious mind. This allows you to engage without tripping defences.

Exercise:

Try this next time you approach someone: come with the mindset of not selling at all. Relax your body language, soften your tone, and avoid any salesy language. Notice how they respond. Are they more engaged? Do they seem relaxed? These responses are your indicators that you're successfully operating within their comfort zone.

As you progress through the book, you'll find more ways to test these exercises, each aimed at making you more attuned to the subtle cues people give off and guiding you to create a seamless connection.

The Power of Softness in Face-to-Face Sales

In a screen-dominated world, face-to-face sales may feel like a lost art. People are so accustomed to online interactions that a genuine human presence- someone who connects- can catch them off guard. There's a power in that softness, in presenting yourself as a person first, salesperson second. By mastering these instincts, you're building an approach that doesn't feel like sales. It feels natural, fluid, human. Once you're equipped with the tools from the upcoming chapters, you'll understand how these instincts form the backbone of every face-to-face interaction. You'll find yourself less of a 'salesperson' and more of a trusted ally, guiding others toward a decision that feels as natural to them as it does to you.

Chapter - 3
Understanding Proximity and Creating Connection

Theme: Activating the Archaic Brain to Build Trust in Close Proximity

Introduction: Why Close Proximity is a Game-Changer

Most people feel a subtle discomfort when someone they don't know steps into their personal space, but the truth is, that proximity can be incredibly powerful when approached correctly. Our brain's ancient wiring is always in action, instinctively scanning for a friend or enemy, especially when someone's close. But here's the thing: if you know how to work with this instinct, you can shift the interaction before they even realize what's happening.

'Where your feet point often shows where your focus lies.'

The Archaic Brain's Reaction to Closeness: Friend or Enemy?

For our ancestors, anyone who stepped into close proximity was either a friend or an enemy- there was no in-between. In a small tribe, that closeness was a survival mechanism, helping people band together against threats or repel those who weren't trustworthy. Even now, the minute you step close to someone, that ancient 'radar' goes off, silently analyzing who you are and what you want.

If you can manage this first moment and understand how to slip past the friend-or-enemy response, then you're already halfway to a meaningful connection. In Chapter 4, we'll explore specific ways to create an immediate, lasting impression that disarms, rather than alarms people.

'Humans Are Kind To Each Other But Ruthless to Salespeople.'

The Non-Threatening Approach: Warmth and Presence

Imagine you walk into a shop. The person behind the counter glances up, not expecting much beyond a 'salesman pitch.' But instead of presenting yourself as a salesperson, you use a soft, natural approach. You're giving off a vibe that says, "I'm just another person, like you" In that moment, you can change their perspective. You can activate the same warm instincts that were once reserved for close allies.

Using proximity to create comfort requires you to ease into their space without making it feel as if you're intruding. Maintain a relaxed body language, a soft tone, and a slight smile. We'll get into the specifics of this 'soft entry' later.

> **'Be in the warm end of the pool, not the cold one.'**

Creating Connection Without Triggering Defences

Think back to the swimming pool analogy: the warm end versus the cold end. When you come on too strong, even if it's friendly, it can make people retreat to the 'cold end' of the metaphorical 'pool of defensiveness.' But if you maintain a gentle, neutral presence, you allow them to ease into the warm end, where they feel more open to connection.

Here's where your awareness of the person's state- their comfort, how guarded they are, their distraction level- plays a crucial role. If you notice defensiveness or hesitation, pause. Keep your energy calm and give them the space to feel comfortable in the moment. By Chapter 8, we'll delve into ways to offer value without taking anything, further reinforcing this comfortable zone you're creating.

Understanding the 'Blind Spots' of Proximity

Just as our hunter-gatherer ancestors knew how to approach animals from the 'blind side' to avoid startling them, we, too, have blind spots in our perception. Humans are hard-wired to have these 'mental blind spots,' and they're especially active in sales settings. If someone steps into their 'salesperson alert zone,' defences shoot up before any real interaction has begun. But if you approach gently, operating within the blind spots of these defences, you can reach the individual without setting off alarms.

Exercise: Use Proximity Blind Spots

Try this when you're next in a face-to-face scenario: move in a way that isn't direct or confrontational. Approach the customer at a slight angle, not directly head-on. When you speak, keep your tone soft and your words casual, almost like you're just there for a chat. Notice how this creates a space of comfort where the person is more likely to open up. Later, when we cover calibration techniques, you'll learn how to adjust on the fly based on subtle cues, making these moves instinctive.

Shortcuts to Trust

- **Avoid over-explaining:** Manage with 4 words instead of 7. People often fall into the trap of overselling, but trust isn't built with a flood of information. It's created through clarity and ease. For instance, instead of listing every feature of a product, focus on one key benefit that matters to the customer. Let them lead the conversation to uncover more.

- **Don't chase; let them come to you:** Keep it light. Confidence means not being overly invested in the outcome of a single interaction. If you're calm and assured, customers feel safe exploring what you're offering. Desperation triggers suspicion, while confidence invites curiosity.

- **Neutral yet relatable presence:** Be specific, but not memorable, this might sound counterintuitive, but it reflects the importance of balance. You want to stand out just enough to be approachable but not so much that your presence overshadows the product. In sales, it's not about you; it's about how your customer feels in your presence. The customer does not remember what you said after you have left but they will remember how you made them feel.

Breaking the Sales Stereotype

Most people's defences go up the moment they sense a 'salesperson' frame. Why? Because they expect pressure, manipulation, or tricks. The techniques you've just learned aren't about hiding who you are- they're about *redefining* what it means to sell. When you step into an interaction with congruence, confidence, and simplicity, you move from being perceived as 'just another salesperson' to someone you trust and enjoy interacting with and another human who has bills to pay.

This isn't about convincing someone to buy; it's about creating an environment where they feel comfortable making that choice themselves.

A Tool, not a Trick

It's important to note that this advice is a tool, not a trick. The intent matters. If your goal is manipulation, customers will pick up on it. But if your goal is to connect, offer value, and make their life better, these principles work naturally. Think of it as stepping into their world and showing them how what you're offering fits seamlessly into it.

Applying These Concepts to Sales: Creating Trust in Seconds

Once you've mastered the skill of creating comfort in close proximity, you'll notice the powerful effect it has. A customer who might otherwise brush you off becomes receptive. The instinctive guard drops, and for a brief moment, you've become more than just a stranger—you're now someone they can trust, even if they don't know exactly why.

> **'Approach as a person, not as a salesperson.'**

Chapter - 4
The 30-Seconds Sales Interaction

> *'Playfulness Isn't About Logic- It's an Emotional Connection Made Through Energy, Recognition, And Rapport.'*

Theme: Breaking Down Each Second to Create a Lasting Impression

Introduction: Why 30 Seconds?

Imagine you've got only 30 seconds to convince someone you're worth listening to. It's a high-stakes situation- where only the right moves make the difference between an instant connection or a flat-out rejection. But here's the thing: it doesn't take a miracle; it takes technique. Each second matters.

Broadcasting and Tuning In: Understanding the Power of Subtle Signals

Before we dive into the details, let's introduce a powerful concept: 'broadcasting.' Here's the idea: when people start speaking, they're constantly broadcasting signals, like radio waves. They may not even realize it, but their choice of words, body language, tone, and even seemingly trivial comments all reveal something about their state of mind, their interests, or their comfort level.

> **'In the first 5 seconds, create curiosity, not suspicion.'**

Picture it like this: they're tuning in to their own 'station,' sharing pieces of information as they speak. If you're attuned, you can pick up on these signals, just like tuning a radio to the right frequency. But if you're even slightly out of sync, like a radio with poor reception, you might miss those hints altogether. And here's the key- if you're paying close attention, you'll spot little 'hooks' in their words, subtle clues that you can pick up on to deepen the connection.

As you go through each phase of these 30 seconds, this 'broadcasting' concept becomes essential. Listen for those hooks- whether it's a comment on the weather, a mention of their store, or a quick observation about the product you're showing. Anything they say can be a clue to their personality, interests, or mood. The more you pick up on these hooks, the more you can adapt your approach to align with their vibe, making the conversation feel organic and comfortable.

'A distracted mind can't see what's coming; use subtle hooks.'

The Breakdown: Every 5 Seconds Counts

Here's the flow of a perfect 30-second interaction, divided into crucial 5-second phases. Each phase serves a specific purpose guiding the customer towards a 'something else ' frame, moving away from 'salesperson frame' and into a comfortable, engaging space.

0-5 Seconds: The Distraction

The first five seconds are all about distraction. This might sound odd, but remember, humans are pattern-seeking creatures. If you walk into a shop and say, "Hi, I'm here to sell…"-bam! You're immediately in the 'sales frame.' Instead, a small, unusual statement (like asking about parking, as I once did, or bringing up a seemingly unrelated and strange topic) works wonders. People expect a certain script from salespeople, and the moment you break that, they're intrigued. This is where the 'something else' frame starts. Want an example? I once opened with, "I'm just here looking for a parking spot," which threw the shopkeeper off, breaking the typical 'salesman' defense straight away.

Real-Life Examples of 5-Second Openers

These openers are moments where humour, curiosity, or a sharp observation helped me connect instantly. Each one is inspired by the setting and the people, designed to ease defences and spark engagement.

The Airlock Mystery

Location: Jewellery Quarter, Birmingham, England, UK

"Wow, this shop has an airlock! Do you guys keep oxygen tanks here or is there some secret ventilation system I should know about?"

Birmingham's Jewellery Quarter is famous for its high-security shops with double-door systems. Walking into one of these shops, I turned the intimidating setup into a light-hearted joke. The owner burst out laughing, and suddenly, the 'salesman' frame was gone.

The Peacock Connection

Location: Indian Jeweller, Jewellery Quarter, Birmingham, England, UK

"I've got peacocks today! And you know, India's national bird is the peacock, so I thought it'd be a perfect fit."

This opener came to me as I noticed the shop owner's Indian heritage. By tapping into a cultural symbol, I instantly created a sense of familiarity. It wasn't just about selling silver animals which I was carrying at the time; it was about making a meaningful connection.

Free Parking Wonders

Location: Marlborough Town, England, UK

"Can you believe it? This town has two hours of free parking! Which affluent English town offers that these days?"

In Marlborough, a town known for its beauty but also its high cost of living, free parking is a rarity. My cheeky comment about this unexpected perk resonated with the shop owner, making them laugh and engage before I even introduced myself.

The Hidden Gem

Location: Marlborough Town, England, UK

"How did I miss this shop? I've driven through this town many a times, but wow, what a gem you've got here!"

Driving through Marlborough, I walked into a charming boutique and offered this enthusiastic opener. Complimenting their shop was genuine, and it instantly made the owner beam with pride.

The Confused Driver Routine

Location: Various Towns Across the UK

"Oh, I was driving to… no, I'm driving… wait, actually, I'm driving for… no, sorry, I was driving to somewhere, but then I thought I'd stop here!"

This intentional stumbling creates intrigue. The shop owner's curiosity is provoked, and the light-hearted confusion shifts their focus away from 'another salesperson' to 'What's this about?'

The Perfect Display Compliment

Location: A Boutique in the Cotswolds, UK

"Your shop has one of the best displays I've ever seen! Do you do it yourself, or do you hire a designer?"

People take pride in their work, and this shop owner in the Cotswolds was no exception. By admiring their genuine creativity, I tapped into a personal connection before mentioning my product.

The Drop-In Neighbour

Location: Various Small Towns Across England, UK

"I was in your town, driving past, and thought I'd drop in and say hello!"

This casual opener makes it seem like I'm not there to sell but to explore. It's disarming and creates a sense of approachability, making it easier to start a conversation.

> **'Don't sell to the customer; motivate them to buy.'**

5-10 Seconds: The Pitch—and Expecting 'No'

In the next five seconds, your job is to give a simple pitch- something brief that gets to the point without sounding pushy. And here's the key: expect a "no." This might seem counterintuitive but hear me out. Most people's reflexive answer is "no" when approached by a salesperson. So, you keep your pitch light, almost offhand. When I said, "I'm selling meerkats," I knew it would prompt curiosity or even a laugh, but I didn't push. I wasn't demanding a yes, and that makes people feel at ease.

If they say no, you're ready to shift tactics. (More about this later.)

10-15 Seconds: False Time Constraint

Now, we introduce a 'false time constraint.' This is where you hint that you're on your way out. It's like a pressure release, easing the person's defences by signalling that you're not there to waste their time. You might say, "I'm just about to go, but I'd love your quick opinion…" At this moment, your body language should back you up: a slight step away, a relaxed posture, and an easy tone, like you really could just walk out.

> 'An authentic smile can open doors faster than the best sales pitch.'

15-20 Seconds: The Appraisal Request

This is where you engage them by asking for a simple opinion. "Could you just give me a quick thought on this product?" Here, you're indirectly asking them to participate. When people offer an opinion, they become subtly invested in the interaction. They're not just being 'sold to' - they're now involved. This taps into a powerful psychological effect: people feel valued when asked for input. And in a few seconds, they've gone from dismissive to curious.

20-25 Seconds: The Product Reveal

At this point, you have to be ready. Whatever you're offering should be easy to show- no fumbling, no searching. When I pull out a piece of jewellery, it's within reach, almost like it's no big deal. This casualness keeps the interaction feeling light and keeps you in the 'something else' frame. Here, the focus is less on 'selling' and more on 'sharing.'

Exercise: Try this reveal technique in a safe environment with friends. Take a product, even if it's just a trinket, and practice a smooth, natural 'reveal.' Get comfortable showing it casually, with a light touch. By practicing this, you'll become so comfortable that when it will be time to do it for real, it'll flow without a hitch.

25-30 Seconds: Creating a Moment of Connection

The final five seconds are about connection. This is where the 'broadcasting' concept comes fully into play. By this point, they've already started to reveal parts of their personality, even if it's just through a quick comment or a glance. Pay attention here- it's all about listening carefully and 'tuning in' to whatever they're broadcasting.

Chapter - 5
Frames and the 'Something Else' Frame

Picture this: You've invited a few friends over for dinner. You're all having a great time- good food, a bottle of wine, laughs all around. The night is winding down, and everyone's starting to gather their things. Then, right as they're about to leave, you casually say, "Oh, by the way, that'll be £30 each."

Imagine the looks on their faces! It would be like you had just dropped a bomb. One moment, they're in a warm, friendly 'we're all mates' frame, and the next, you've flipped it to "wait, what?" Suddenly, you're not their friend hosting a lovely dinner. You're a restaurant server asking for the bill. Awkward wouldn't even begin to cover it.

That's the power of frames. A frame is like the setting or the lens through which we view any interaction. Shift the frame, and the whole vibe changes instantly.

> **'No one wants their frame shifted unexpectedly.'**

Why Does This Matter in Sales?

In sales, especially face-to-face, the way people view you- the frame they put you in- determines how they'll respond. If they peg you as a typical salesperson, they'll be on guard, saying "no" before you even get a word in. But if you surprise them, step out of that 'salesperson' frame, and into the 'something else' frame, they're intrigued. They'll drop their defences, relax, and open up.

> **'The 'something else' frame disarms defences and invites connection.'**

The Three Frames in Customer Interactions

When you meet someone new in a selling situation, they usually categorize you in one of three ways:

1. **The Friend Frame:** "Do I know this person?"

Think of this like the dinner-with-friends frame. Here, there's trust and warmth. But with strangers, it's rare to start here unless you're a personal referral.

2. **The Sales Frame:** "Oh no, they're trying to sell me something."

This is the default. People assume any stranger trying to engage them is just out to make a sale. This frame makes them guarded and defensive. Think of it as them pulling up the mental shutters.

3. **The 'Something Else' Frame:** "Hmm, what's this person's deal?"

This is the golden ticket. When you step out of the typical sales frame and into the 'something else' frame, you catch people off guard in a good way. They're curious, engaged, and willing to listen.

Creating the 'Something Else' Frame: The Dinner Party Lesson

So, how do you create this 'something else' frame?

Let's go back to the dinner party example. Your friends expected a friendly, social evening, but the minute you switched it to a transaction- wham! -they were jolted into a different frame, and it felt awkward and unnatural.

In sales, you can do the reverse. Instead of letting customers slot you straight into the 'salesperson' role, you start with something unexpected, light-hearted, or simply human. They're bracing for the usual sales pitch, but instead, you surprise them with a different approach.

> **'Treat everyone like a good friend and trust will follow.'**

The Importance of Intent: Why It Has to Be Real

You can't fake this. Humans have a sixth sense of insincerity. If you're just 'acting' like you don't care about making the sale, people will pick up on it. But if you genuinely don't mind walking away, that comes through.

This is where the fishing analogy comes in: when you lose a fish, you don't throw a fit. You just cast again, knowing there are plenty more in the water. When you're meeting a customer, adopt the same mindset. You're shouldn't there to reel them in at any cost. You should be genuinely open to seeing if there's a connection- and if not, that's okay.

This attitude doesn't just relax you; it puts the customer at ease too. They can sense when you're not desperate for a sale, and it makes them curious.

Body Language and the 'Something Else' Frame

Creating this 'something else' frame isn't just about what you say- it's about how you carry yourself. Your body language, tone, and facial expressions all matter. Stand a little to the side instead of squarely in front of them. Keep your hands open, and gesture casually as if you're chatting with an old friend.

Imagine you're leaning against a counter, relaxed, rather than standing stiffly, looking eager. Subtly this body language communicates that you're in no rush, that you're genuinely present. You're not here to push a product- you're here to have a conversation.

It's like pressing pause on a mental reflex. Suddenly, they're not sure how to respond. And in that moment of uncertainty, they're open to whatever comes next. This is where you can shift the conversation and show them something new, something human.

Frames Aren't Manipulation—They're Connection

It's easy to think of frames as some kind of psychological trick, but it's not about manipulation. Frames are simply ways to create more genuine connections by understanding how people naturally respond. You're not forcing them into anything. You're just stepping into a frame that lets them relax and be curious.

As we head into Chapter 6, we'll build on this concept by exploring what it means to be 'inside' versus 'outside' your head. This next step is about staying present, letting go of self-consciousness, and engaging with people as they are, not as you want them to be.

Chapter - 6
Inside Your Head vs. Outside Your Head

> 'Trying To Logically Convince Someone To Like You Actually Lessens Their Emotional Response.'

Picture this: You're standing face-to-face with a potential customer, a person who, within seconds, will decide if you're someone they trust- or someone they'd rather avoid. You've got about 30 seconds to make a connection, and every bit of that moment matters. There's a whole psychology at play, one that begins and ends with trust.

Now, here's a bit of truth we all know but rarely think about: people buy from people they like or trust. Liking is often instant, sparked by a smile or a warm introduction. Trust, though? That *usually* takes time.

When you're outside your head, fully present and focused on the other person, it has a powerful effect. People can feel it. This kind of presence is disarming because it makes others feel at ease. They feel that you're engaged, and genuinely tuned in to who they are and what they might need. That comfort creates a sense of safety, and safety is at the root of trust.

> 'True congruence happens when your inner identity and outward actions are fully aligned.'

In contrast, when you're 'inside your head,' everything changes. Imagine trying to listen to someone while constantly worrying about what you'll say next or whether you're coming off right. You're stuck in a loop of self-monitoring and

> 'The truth always shines through; you can't fake authenticity.'

second-guessing, which pulls you out of the moment. This inward focus makes it harder to genuinely engage with the other person. You're there, but you're not *really* there. The energy shifts, and people can feel that disconnection.

The Traits of Inside vs. Outside Your Head

Here's a quick breakdown of the difference between these two states of mind:

Inside Your Head

- Worrying about how you come across.
- Trying to fit in, impress, or entertain.
- Feeling nervous or flustered
- Needing the interaction to go well, fearing it might not.
- Feeling undeserving of others' attention or respect
- Feeling insecure, lacking confidence
- Overthinking every word and gesture
- Fearing judgment or failure
- Feeling stiff or robotic
- Stifling natural reactions and expressions

Outside Your Head

- Comfortable in the moment, without attachment to outcomes
- Attentive and tuned into the other person.
- Relaxed, natural, and organic in your responses.
- Able to listen deeply.
- Confident in who you are, regardless of others' reactions.
- Assured in your value, not needing to prove yourself.
- Free to express humour, honesty, and authenticity.
- Trusting that the interaction will flow naturally.

- Letting go of self-consciousness

- Engaged with the conversation without a rigid agenda.

A James Bond Story: An Illustration of Being Outside Your Head

So, what is a good example of being Outside Your Head? Take James Bond, a super-secret government spy working for MI6. When James Bond is seducing the crime lord's girlfriend, pretending he is at the villain's rooftop party as an accountant, do you think he is looking away from her eyes and fumbling over his words because he is too busy wondering if his posture is suspicious? No. He is confident and intimate. He looks directly into her eyes and doesn't worry about anyone else, if he stays natural no one will find him suspicious.

> **'Your vibe comes from the way your mind processes and expresses emotions.'**

The main difference between James Bond and anyone else (apart from the gunfights and near-death experiences) is that James Bond tries to trick people with his charms and confidence, getting them to do things they don't want to. For anyone else, and you, that is not necessary. You use the same self-confidence and calm, but naturally, genuinely. You shouldn't have to convince someone to talk to you if you are as human and natural as possible. Additionally, the fate of the world is not at stake for you. You can be better than James Bond…

So, when you're outside your head in a sales interaction, you're not second-guessing or overthinking. You're observing, tuned into the other person's signals, and responding in real-time. Like James Bond seeing if the girlfriend has caught on yet, you're able to read subtle cues- eye movements, body language shifts, and tones of voice. You become more like an observer than a participant, letting the interaction flow naturally and adapting as it unfolds.

> **'Your self-concept is always evolving, shaped by your interactions and the feedback you get.'**

This state is where trust-building truly shines. When you're fully present, people feel comfortable around you. You're not giving off that forced 'salesperson' vibe because you're genuinely engaged. You're not pushing for a particular outcome; you're allowing the interaction to develop on its own.

This comfort becomes a foundation for trust, as people instinctively feel safe with someone who's both confident and genuinely present.

Practical Exercise: Step Out and Practice

Now, here's a small exercise to start building this skill. The next time you're in a conversation, make a conscious effort to focus entirely on the other person. Watch for their expressions, their tone, their body language. Set aside any thoughts about what you'll say next or how you're coming across. Just be there with them. Notice how it feels to shift your focus completely, and how the interaction flows when you're not wrapped up in your thoughts.

This is a habit you can strengthen over time. It's not about getting it perfect every time. It's about noticing the difference it makes and building on that. The more you practice being outside your head, the more natural it becomes, and the easier it is to connect with people on a deeper level.

Chapter - 7
Conquering Fear with Core Confidence

Let's start with a simple question: what's the worst that could happen? When you're about to approach someone in sales- or in any interaction, really- that question sits at the back of your mind, doesn't it? That's normal. Fear is that little voice that tells us, "Stay safe. Don't risk rejection." And for most of us, it feels like a solid wall.

But here's a revelation: that fear you're feeling? It's nothing more than an emotional reaction to your thoughts. Fear doesn't live in the situation itself; it's created by the thoughts we attach to it. This means if we change our thoughts, we can change our emotional response. So, instead of a wall, it's more like a thin veil you can see right through with the right tools.

Imagine you're standing on the edge of a diving board. Your body might be screaming, "Don't jump!" But the water below is safe, the jump is short, and thousands have done it before. In sales, this 'diving board' moment happens each time you approach someone new. The key? Getting your mind to stop seeing it as a jump at all.

> **'You are responsible for your own state of mind.'**

Fear is an Emotional Reaction to Thoughts, Not Reality

The clinical truth is that fear is just that- an emotional reaction to your thoughts. Our emotions, as powerful as they are, do not always line up with logic. Emotions are often illogical and impulsive, while thoughts, when guided, can be rational and steadying.

This is why, when you look at the situation logically, most of your fears dissolve. Logically, you know the worst thing that could happen is they say no. That's it. But emotions? They take that no and spin it into a catastrophe.

So, here's where the shift begins. When you are outside your head, you're able to manage fear because you're not overthinking every interaction. The brain stays calm, and your emotions are grounded. And, by the way, this isn't about eliminating fear. It's about recognizing that fear is an instinctive part of you and learning to work with it- not letting it dictate your actions.

> 'How you feel inside will inevitably influence the people around you.'

Situational Confidence vs. Core Confidence

Let's bring in another distinction here: situational confidence versus core confidence. This idea is powerful and incredibly freeing once you get it. Situational confidence depends on the environment, context, or specific roles- like when a manager or a university lecturer seems confident in a meeting or in front of a class but looks lost in a social setting. Their confidence shifts depending on the 'situation.'

Now, core confidence? It's a whole other beast. Core confidence doesn't rely on circumstances. It's the kind of assurance that travels with you into any setting, whether you're pitching a product or standing at a friend's party. This is the state where nothing shakes you. Have you ever seen James Bond phased by anything? What he displays is core confidence no matter what situation he is in. It doesn't matter if someone rejects your pitch, doubts your idea, or questions your worth. Core confidence makes you unshakable because it comes from within- it's not tied to anyone else's approval.

And that's the goal here. When you're operating from core confidence, you're not constantly shifting to 'fit in' with each new scenario. Instead, you walk into every situation with the same energy, knowing that what happens next is just information. You're free from that fear of rejection because you've already decided that no outcome will define you.

The Thermometer vs. Thermostat

Think of your confidence like a thermostat. External events, rejections, or minor failures shouldn't shift it. Just as a thermostat regulates and reads the environment's temperature but isn't affected by it, your confidence should reflect situations without changing your core.

Situational confidence fluctuates, like a thermometer's reading in different climates, but core confidence? That's more like a constant temperature control- it stays steady, regardless of what's going on around you. This steadiness is your strength. When you maintain core confidence, you're unaffected by the little ups and downs in interactions.

Exercise: Building Core Confidence

Here's a simple exercise to start reinforcing your core confidence. Next time you approach someone, pay attention to the thoughts that come up. Are they based on fear of rejection? Do they make you feel 'less than' or like you're not enough?

Now, take a moment to flip the script. Think, "What if their response has nothing to do with my worth?" By separating your self-worth from the outcome, you're already starting to weaken that hold of situational confidence. The more you do this, the more natural it becomes, and soon, those fears will lose their grip.

Chapter - 8
Offering Value Through Genuine Connection

When you walk into a room, what are you offering? It's a question that might seem out of place in the world of sales, but this is the difference between a salesperson and a trusted connection. Are you there to add value—or just to get something out of it? The way you approach this question changes everything.

A lot of people see sales as a numbers game. "Close the deal, make the quota, and move on." But in reality, each interaction is an opportunity to leave a lasting impression, to make someone feel genuinely heard, seen, and valued. This isn't about being manipulative or playing mind games; it's about being fully present, bringing value, and letting go of the outcome.

In a world where people buy from people they like and trust, simply shifting your focus to offer rather than take is a game-changer.

> 'In sales, offering value is the gateway to rapport.'

And there's a reason this works—when someone feels you're not trying to 'get' something from them, their defences naturally come down. They feel comfortable, valued, and more likely to engage. As previously mentioned, it's like casting a line while fishing: you're there to enjoy the experience, knowing there are plenty of fish in the sea, and not stressing over each bite or tug. If you lose one, there's always another. This detachment is key.

The Fishing Analogy: Letting Go of the Outcome

I would like to emphasize this again although I touched on this in previous chapters. Imagine sitting by the edge of a lake, casting a line, and waiting patiently. When the fish nibble but don't bite, you don't throw down your rod in frustration. You know there's always another fish, and you keep casting, relaxed, and easy-going. In sales, this is what I call the 'fishing approach.' The idea is that there's no desperation, no frantic rush to reel in the 'big one.' You're there, casting your line, bringing value, and waiting for the right opportunity to come along. This relaxed state not only puts the customer at ease but also allows you to approach each interaction from a place of abundance rather than scarcity.

In a sales context, this approach is immensely powerful. When a customer senses that you're not desperate for the sale, they feel more comfortable and open around you. They're not dealing with someone who is chasing a commission but rather with a person who's genuinely interested in connecting. And this subtle shift builds a sense of trust and respect that's hard to come by.

> 'We're wired to tune out people who add less value and focus on those who matter more.'

Giving vs. Taking: The Key to Building Rapport

Think about a time when you felt truly connected with someone, when you felt they were interested in you and weren't expecting anything in return. That's the feeling you want to create in a sales interaction. When you give- whether it's a piece of knowledge, a compliment, or simply your undivided attention- you create a small but powerful bond. It's like building a bridge, one piece at a time.

This is where the difference between offering value and taking value becomes crystal clear. Offering value means bringing something to the table, something that enhances the other person's experience, even if they don't buy from you. Taking value is when you're simply there to extract something- a "yes," a credit card, a quick sale.

> 'Genuine connection beats manipulation every time.'

When you're the type of person, who consistently offers value, customers feel it. They remember you; they trust you, and often, they'll come back because they know you're not just there for the transaction. You're there to create a meaningful connection.

The Friend Analogy: Genuine Connections Don't Sell

Here's a concept that's subtle but powerful: as mentioned before, in most cultures, friends don't sell things to each other. Even if they do, they keep it light because the friendship is more valuable than the transaction. That's the feeling you want to generate in your interactions- where the customer feels as comfortable with you as they would with a friend. It doesn't mean being overly familiar or casual; it means showing that you value the relationship more than the sale.

Exercise: Practicing Value-Based Interactions

Here's an exercise to practice this concept. The next time you interact with a potential customer, try this: focus solely on giving. Maybe it's advice, maybe it's a compliment, or maybe it's just your undivided attention. Notice how this changes the feel of the interaction, how the person responds, and how you feel afterward.

This exercise helps you switch from a 'taking' mindset to a 'giving' mindset, which is essential for building genuine rapport. By focusing on what you can offer, you'll see a shift in how customers engage with you. It's as if they can sense the difference, feeling that you're there to enhance their experience, not just your bottom line.

What's Next?

In this chapter, we'll dive deeper into the nuances of body language and presence, and why 95% of what you convey happens without words. You'll learn to spot hidden cues and calibrate your approach naturally, ensuring your 'giving' approach resonates fully. So, keep reading, this is where we take the subtleties of nonverbal communication to a whole new level.

Chapter - 9
Calibration and the Art of 'Being' Over 'Doing'

> 'Most Decisions Happen Unconsciously Through Body Language And Tone of Voice.'

By now, you are starting to see how powerful these subtle changes in approach can be. You are also realizing that the final key isn't just about knowing these techniques but about letting them become second nature. This is where we step beyond the mechanics of sales and get into something deeper: the art of being.

Most people approach sales with a mindset of doing- strategizing, executing, and 'making things happen.' But what if I told you that the real mastery lies in being rather than doing? When you're just being, everything flows more naturally. It's no longer an act or a series of tactics you apply one by one; it's who you are. And, believe me, people can feel the difference. When you reach this stage, there's an almost magical shift that happens.

> **'To know is to be. Mastery means internalizing, not pretending.'**

'Being' is Effortless: Why Calibration is 95% Body Language

Calibration is the art of adjusting in real-time without consciously trying. It's not about reacting but about responding in a way, that feels instinctive and organic. Calibration happens automatically when you're present, deeply tuned into the other person, and aligned within yourself. You're not calculating or planning; you're simply being in the moment.

When you're operating from this state, 95% of what you convey is in your body language, and only 5% comes down to words. Your tone, your posture, the way you look someone in the eye, and even the micro-expressions you may not notice- all these elements combine to broadcast something essential: "I am here, fully present, and I see you."

> **'Your thoughts and behaviours are in constant interplay, subtly shaping one another.'**

If you're outside your head, if you're genuinely focused on the other person, your subconscious mind will naturally guide you to say and do the right things. It's like the internal calibration is happening without conscious effort, thanks to the depth of your understanding and presence.

The Shortcut to Trust: Why 'Being' Feels Safe

When you're fully being in the moment, people pick up on it immediately. There's no sense of manipulation or hidden agenda. You're simply there, offering value, and this creates a shortcut to trust. In previous chapters, we discussed the psychology behind this: how, for most of human history, close proximity to another person automatically led to one of two conclusions- friend or enemy.

When you're not trying to force the outcome, you project a non-threatening, friendly presence. This is where the 'shortcut to trust' comes into play, built on a foundation of comfort and safety.

> **'Authenticity is the balance between who you are, what you believe, and how you express it.'**

The Slow-Motion Perception: Seeing the World Differently

At this point, you can practice picking up on subtle cues and anticipate reactions, allowing you to respond with finesse. This isn't about reading people's minds; it's about being so in tune with what's happening that you can navigate the conversation smoothly.

For example, imagine you're in a sales pitch, and the customer starts to frown slightly or cross their arms. You pick up on these cues and adjust. Maybe you soften your tone, lean back, or shift the conversation slightly. The adjustment is seamless because you're not actively thinking, "I need to do X to get Y." Instead,

> **'Your voice is the ultimate reflection of who you are.'**

you're just responding instinctively, reading the situation without forcing it.

Exercise: The Art of Relaxed Focus

Here's a final exercise to practice letting go of the 'doing' and embracing the art of 'being.' The next time you're in a conversation, focus on the other person completely. Don't think about what you'll say next or how to steer the conversation. Simply listen. Allow your body language and words to respond naturally, without a set goal in mind. Notice how the interaction changes when you shift from doing to being.

This might sound simple, but it's one of the hardest things to master. Yet, once you've got it, this skill will set you apart in ways you can't imagine.

What's Next?

In the concluding chapter, we'll pull all these threads together, giving you a final roadmap to approach face-to-face interactions with confidence and purpose. As you step into this new way of 'being,' remember that it's not about perfection; it's about presence. So, hang on-you're about to see how all these pieces come together to create something truly transformative.

Conclusion
Bridging the Archaic and the Modern with Heart

We began this journey by traveling back to the roots of humanity, to a time when our ancestors operated in small tribes, relying on instincts and survival skills honed over thousands of years. Those ancient, archaic brains- wired for instant decision-making, seeking safety, forming bonds, and finding allies- are still very much alive within us today. It's almost surreal: though we've built towering cities, connected the globe digitally, and expanded our minds with knowledge, our brains remain grounded in those primal roots.

The Archaic Brain in the Modern World

Every day, we carry this prehistoric brain into the world, navigating a complex society filled with technology, rapid change, and constant information. Our brains were not designed to sift through a deluge of emails or to 'swipe right' on potential friends. They're still calibrated to operate in a world where survival is about face-to-face interactions, detecting threats, and forming bonds based on trust and familiarity.

> **'Every interaction is an opportunity, not a transaction.'**

Here's the challenge: our environment has changed at light speed, but our brain's underlying structure has not. We still react to people and situations through these ancient filters, and they colour how we make decisions, build trust, and form connections. This isn't just a theory; it's a reality you can observe every day. Think about it: we feel more connected to someone in person than over a screen. Our instincts tell us that people who show up, stand beside us, and speak with us face-to-face are more trustworthy. That's why, even in a world filled with digital shortcuts, the ancient art of face-to-face connection holds unparalleled power.

The essence of business should be done with your heart. It's not about transactions; it's about building relationships that last. Think about those ancient tribes, where trust was not just a preference but a necessity for survival. If someone in the tribe gave value without expecting an immediate return, they were considered an asset. Likewise, when we approach sales with the intent to offer genuine value rather than simply 'making a sale,' we activate that same sense of belonging, safety, and trust.

'Good business is done with heart and authenticity.'

This doesn't just benefit the individual interaction; it secures the entire relationship. Business done with heart creates a bond that withstands the competitive, often cutthroat world we live in. It's not transactional- it's relational. People will return to you, not because they have to, but because they want to. And that's a connection far more powerful and secure than anything built on a quick sale or clever pitch.

The Final 30 Seconds

As you close this book and prepare to step into the world with the skills you've learned, remember that what makes these tools truly powerful isn't the techniques themselves- it's how you use them. At their core, these principles are about creating connections rooted in authenticity, simplicity, and trust.

In a world full of noise, *cognitive simplicity* is your greatest ally. People crave clarity. When you strip away the unnecessary and focus on what matters, you make it easier for others to connect with you. Don't overthink. Don't over-explain. Simplicity- transparency, is powerful. It clears a path to trust and leaves room for the customer to make their own decisions without pressure.

To sum it up, here's a piece of advice from a film script that resonates deeply: "Don't use seven words when four will do. Don't shift your weight. Be specific but not memorable. Be funny but don't make them laugh. They've got to like you and then forget you the moment you've left their side."

It may have been written for a fictional character, but the truth beneath it is universal. Keep things simple, stay genuine, and leave people feeling good in your presence. In sales- and in life- that's all you really need.

Raj Adgopul

www.ingramcontent.com/pod-product-compliance
Lightning Source LLC
La Vergne TN
LVHW061604070526
838199LV00077B/7163